BASIC SPANISH PHRASES

Pedro & Pete

BY BOBBY BASIL

LISTEN HOW TO SAY THE WORDS!

You can listen at spanishtoenglishpodcast.com, iTunes, or Spotify!

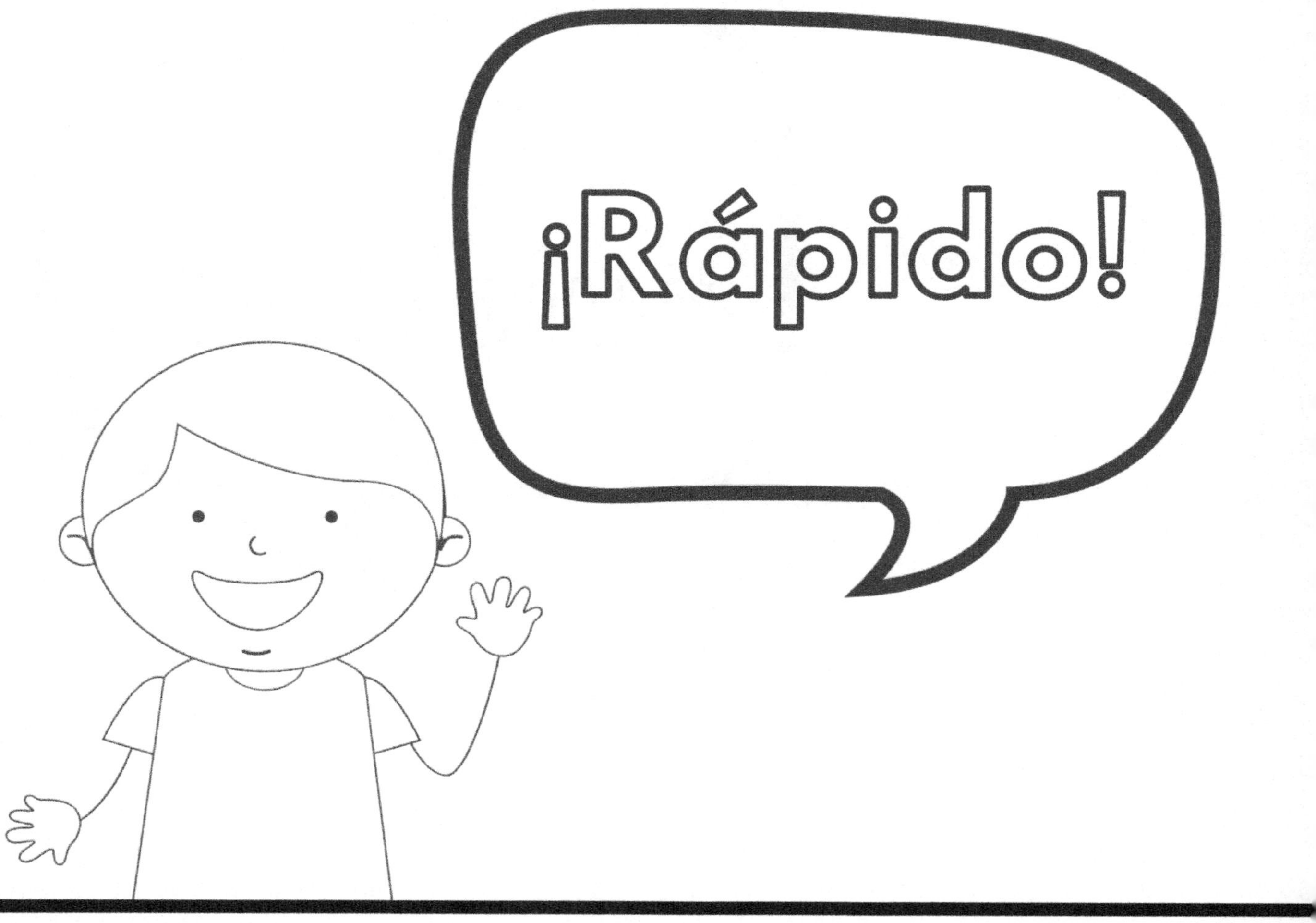
¡Rápido!

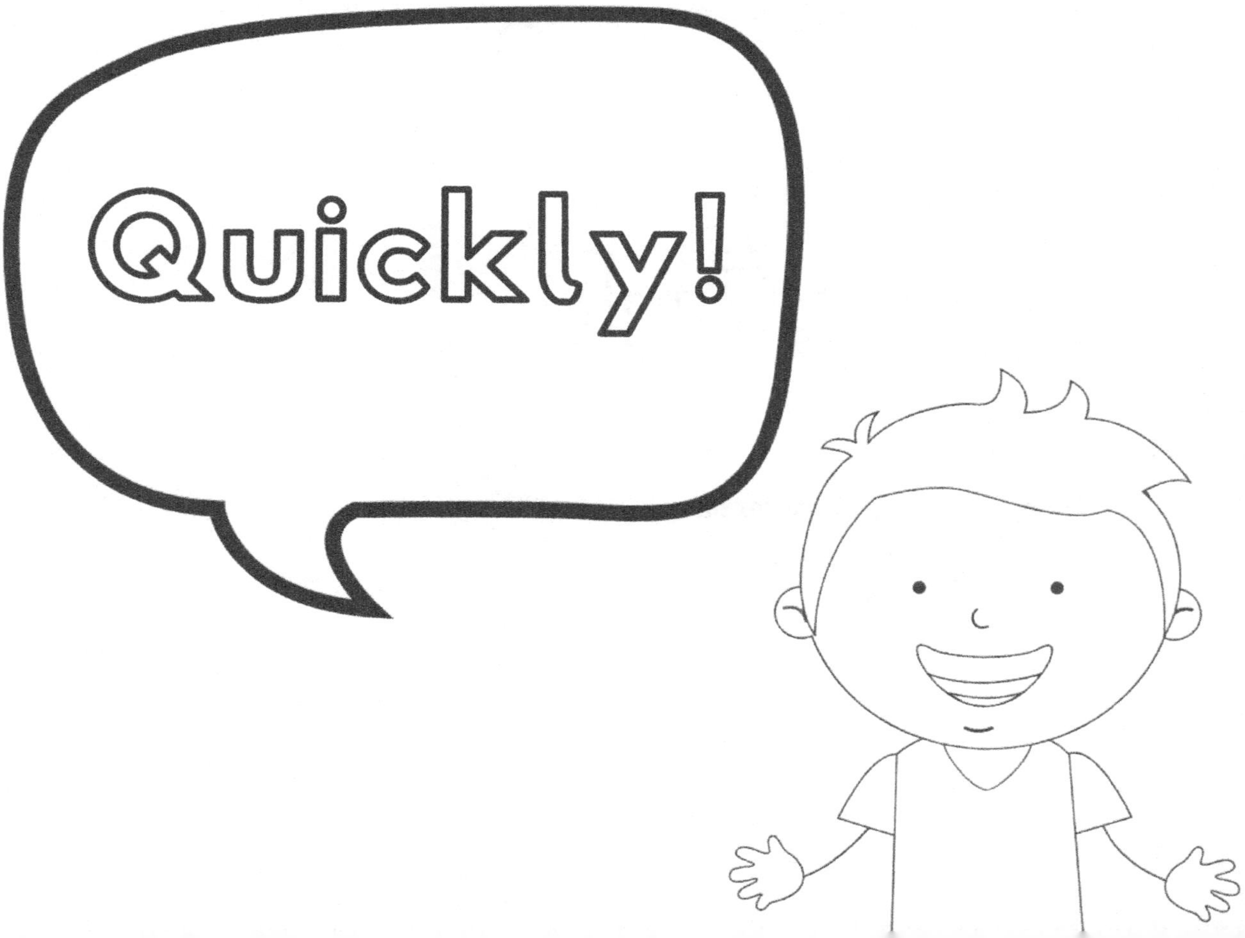
Quickly!

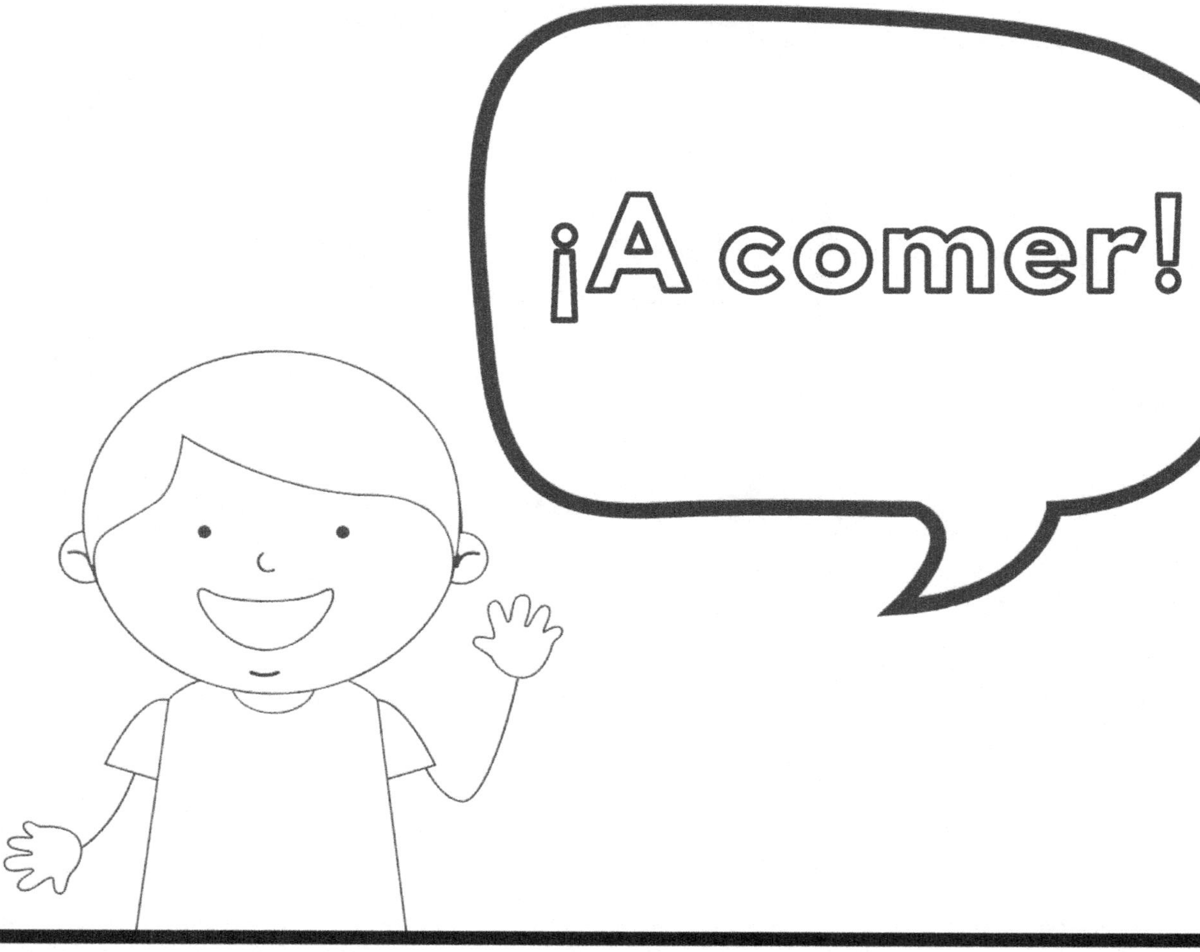
¡A comer!

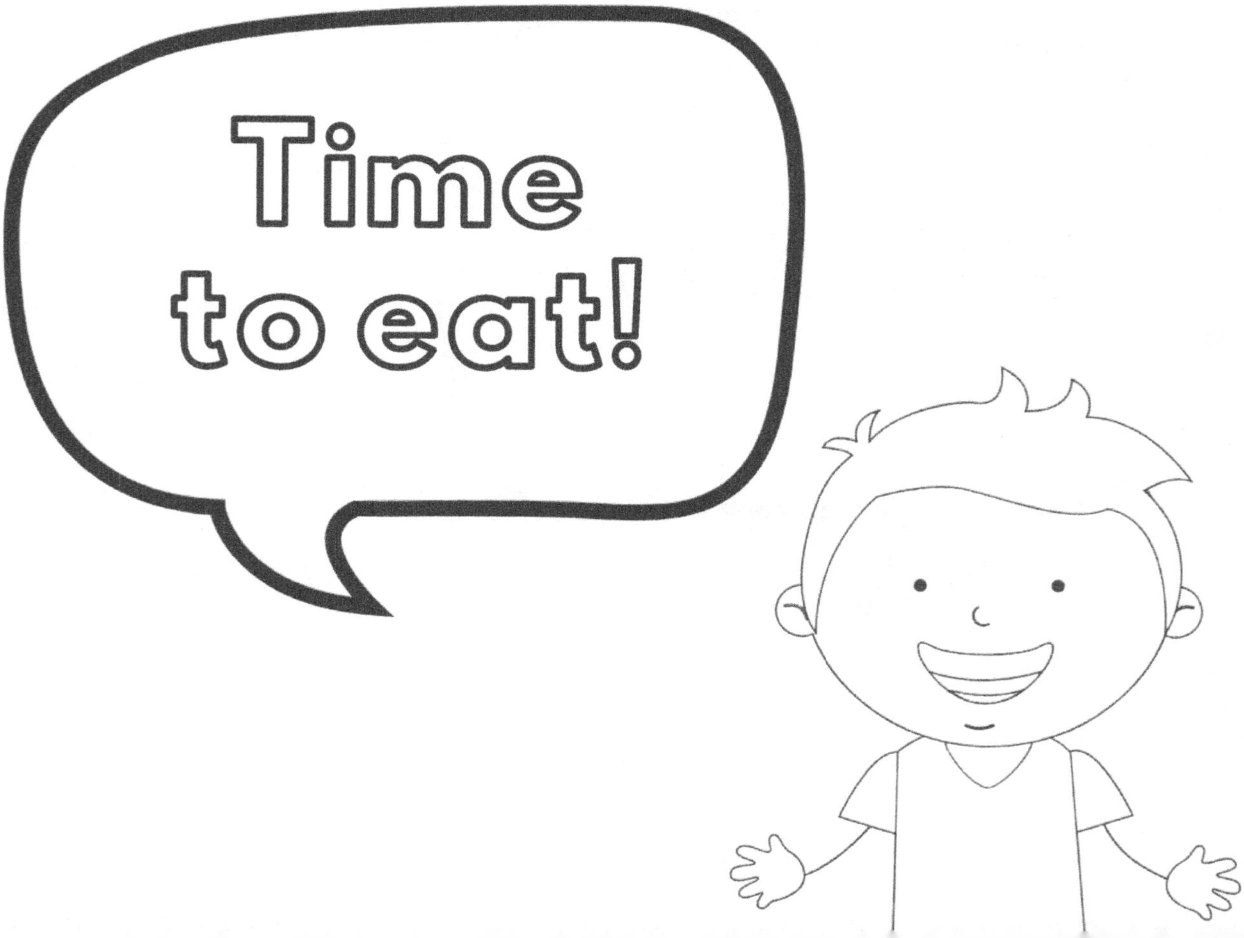
Time to eat!

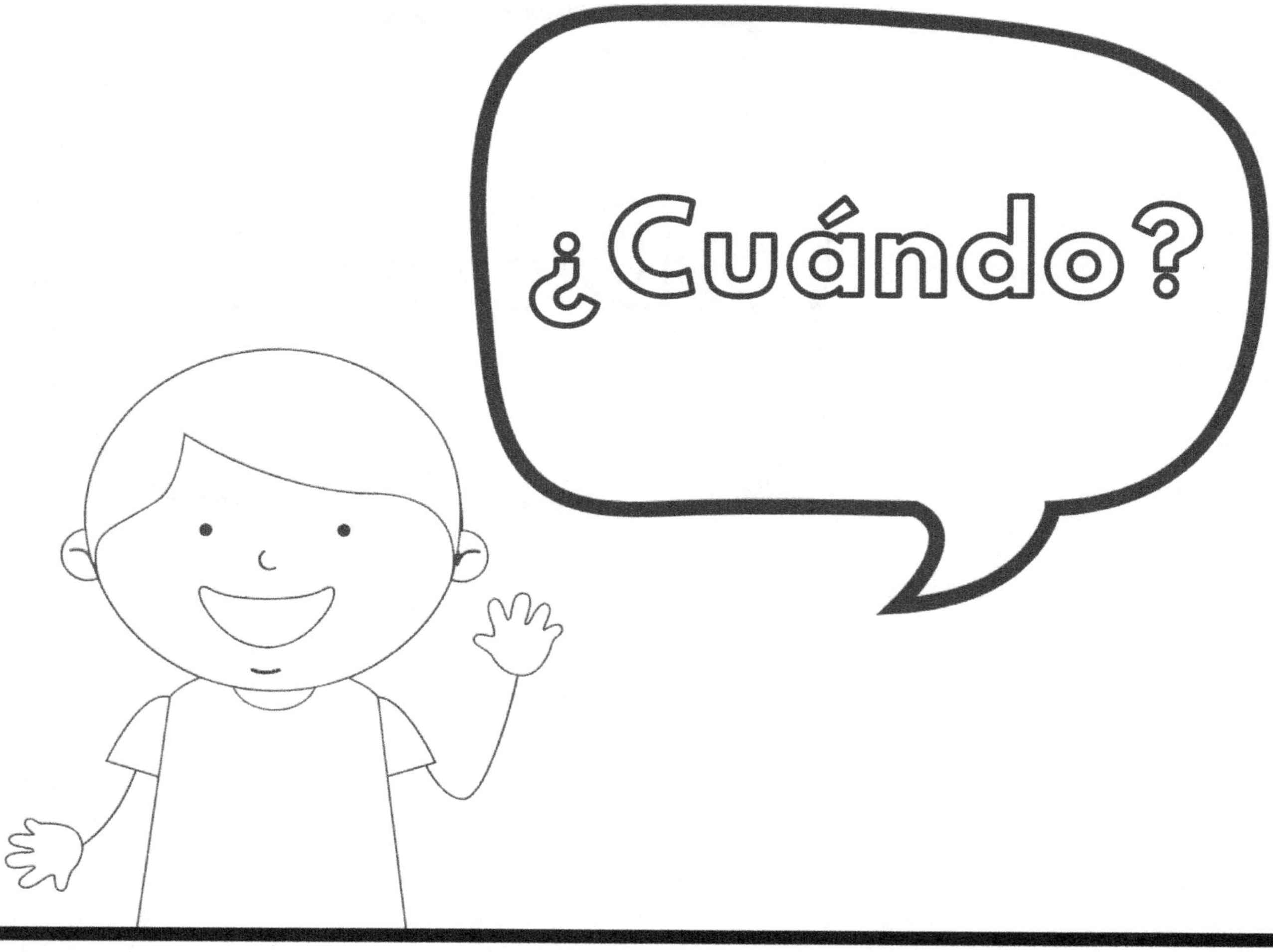
¿Cuándo?

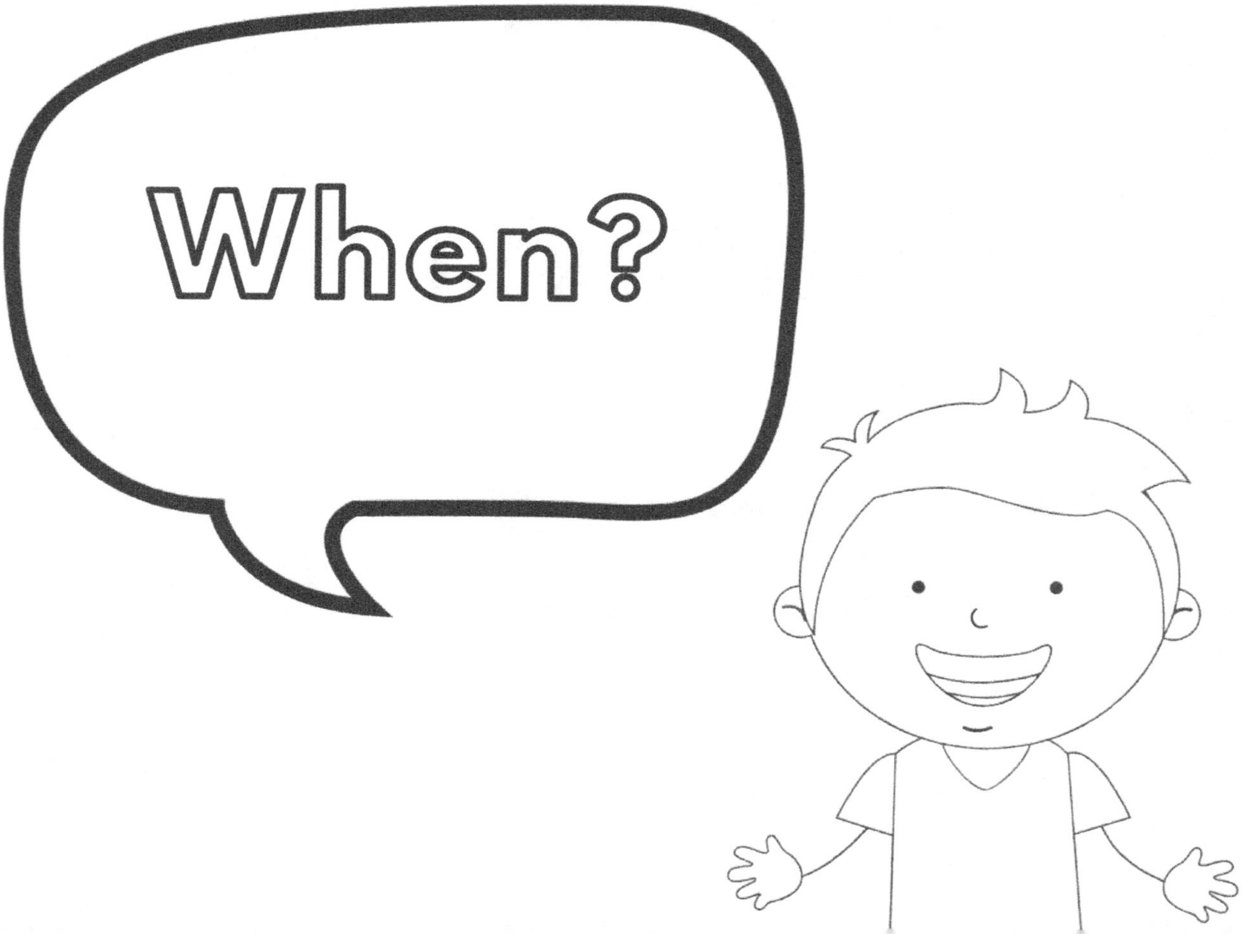
When?

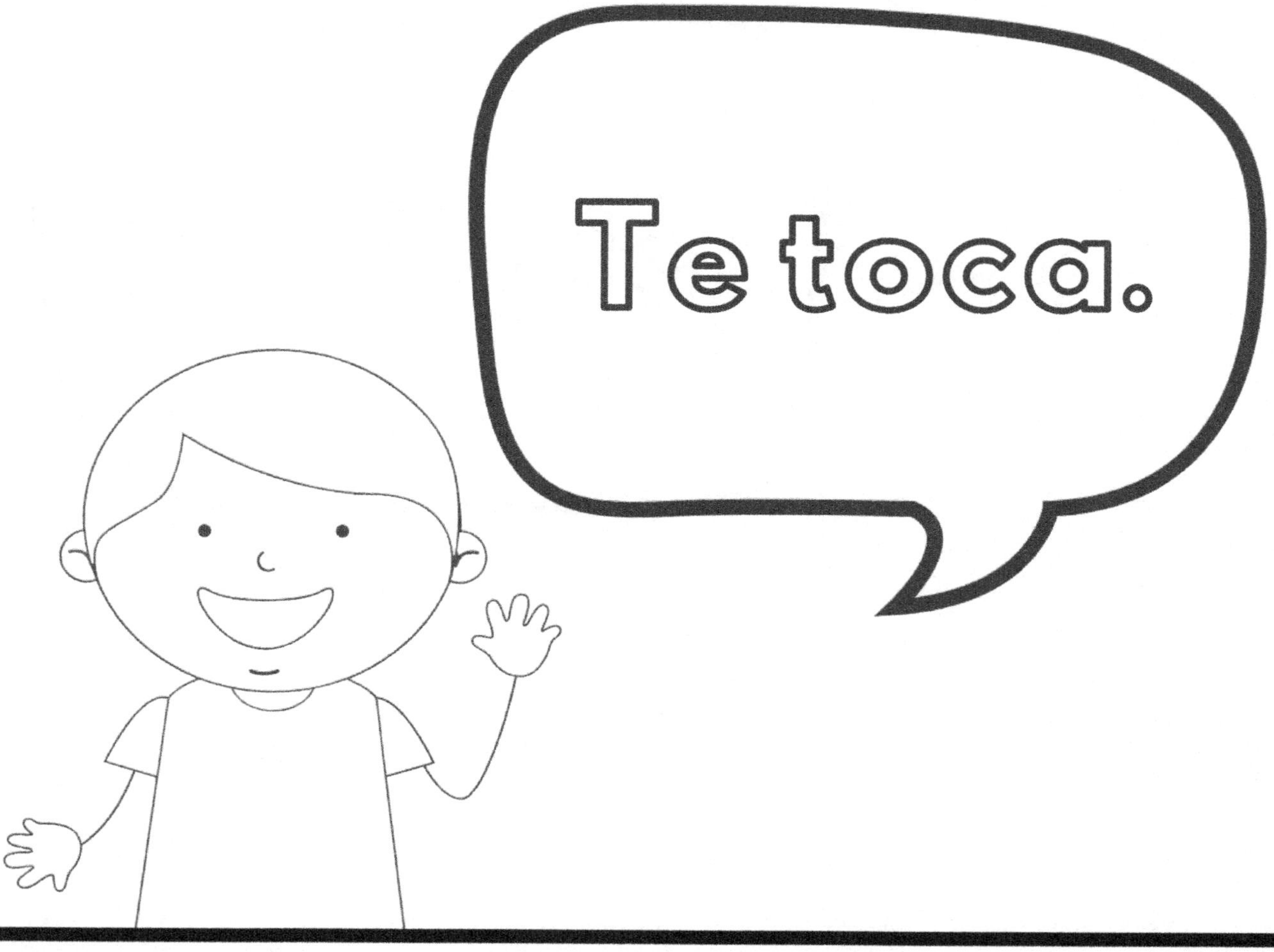
Te toca.

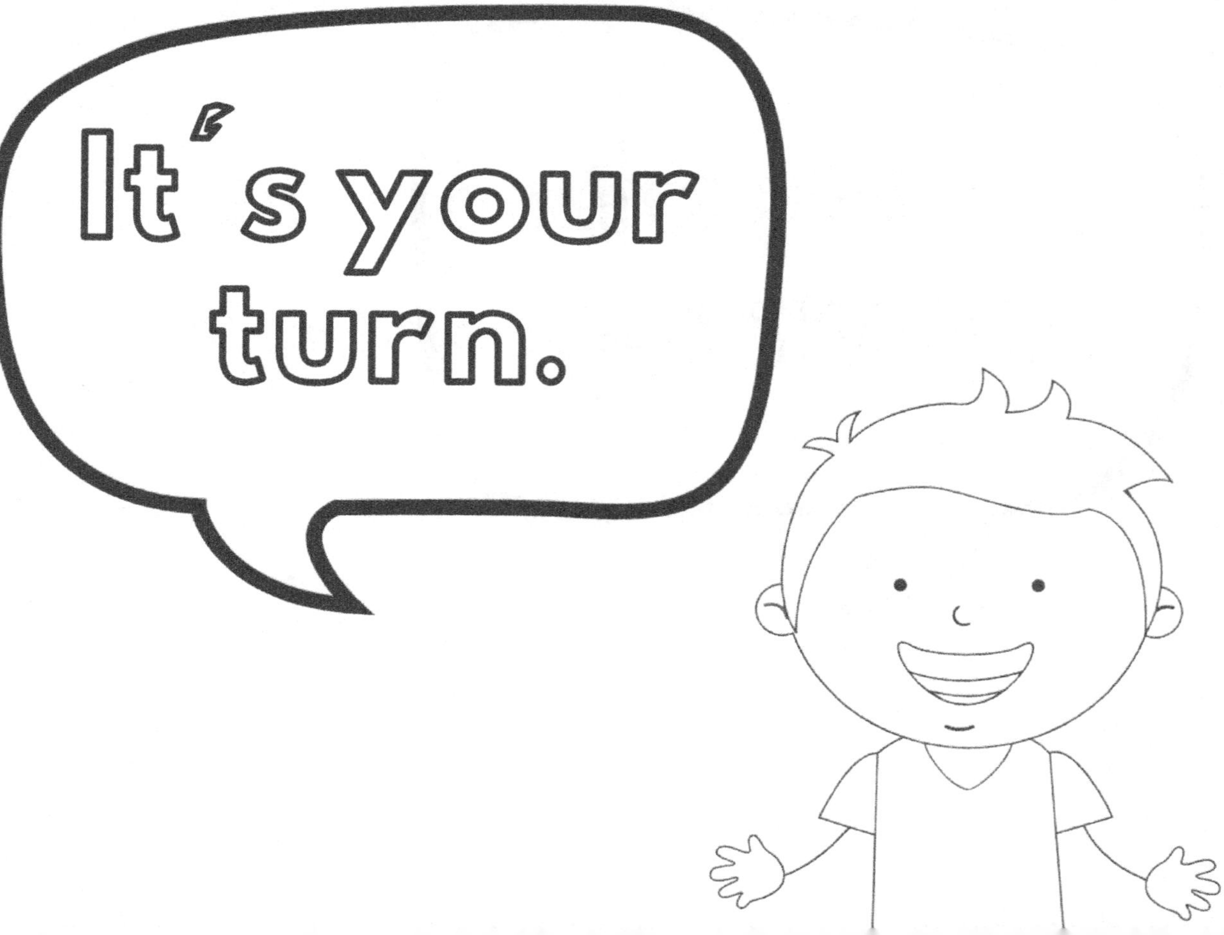
It´s your turn.

PLEASE
LEAVE A REVIEW
ON AMAZON!

Your review will
help other readers
discover my books.
Thank you!

Made in the USA
Monee, IL
16 September 2020